# WHAT'S YOUR SUPERPOWER?

QUIZ EVER

By Brooke Rowe

Published in the United States of America by Cherry Lake Publishing
Ann Arbor, Michigan
www.cherrylakepublishing.com

Reading Adviser: Marla Conn MS, Ed., Literacy specialist, Read-Ability, Inc.
Book Designer: Melinda Millward

Photo Credits: ©William Perugini/Shutterstock.com, back cover, 4; ©monkeybusinessimages/Thinkstock.com, back cover, 4; ©xubingruo/Thinkstock.com, cover, 1; ©Thinkstock/Thinkstock.com, 6; ©Jacob Ammentorp Lund/Thinkstock.com, 6; ©Digital Vision/Thinkstock.com, 7; ©Creatas Images/Thinkstock.com, 7; ©BluIz60/Thinkstock.com, 8; ©Jorge Casais/Shutterstock.com, 8; ©Monkey Business Images/Shutterstock.com, 9, 21; ©pirita/Shutterstock.com, 9; ©katalinks/CanStock, 10; ©Andy Nowack/Dreamstime.com, 10; ©Nicole Abalde/http://www.flickr.com/CC BY-ND 2.0, 11; ©Steven Leon Day/Shutterstock.com, 11; ©Ermolaev Alexander/Shutterstock.com, 12; ©kawing921/Shutterstock.com, 12; ©Jacek Chabraszewski/Shutterstock.com, 13; ©KWSPhotography/Shutterstock.com, 13; ©jean-marie guyon/Thinkstock.com, 14; ©Landd09/Dreamstime.com, 14; ©Jupiterimages/Thinkstock.com, 15, 18, 26; ©Dndavis/Dreamstime.com, 15; ©Eugene Sergeev/Shutterstock.com, 16; ©Kues/Shutterstock.com, 16; ©Joggie Botma/Shutterstock.com, 17; ©janecat/Shutterstock.com, 17; ©Benoit Daoust/Shutterstock.com, 18; ©muzsy/Shutterstock.com, 19; ©Martin Novak/Shutterstock.com, 19; ©CREATISTA/Shutterstock.com, 20; ©Siberia - Video and Photo/Shutterstock.com, 20; ©Linn Currie/Shutterstock.com, 21; ©PeopleImages/iStockphoto, 22; ©Rocketclips, Inc./Shutterstock.com, 22; ©Mitrofanov Alexander/Shutterstock.com, 23; ©Rich Carey/Shutterstock.com, 23; ©Prasit Rodphan/Shutterstock.com, 24; ©Corepics VOF/Shutterstock.com, 24; ©michaeljung/Thinkstock.com, 25; ©Kuznetsov Alexey/Shutterstock.com, 25; ©Lolostock/Shutterstock.com, 26; ©l i g h t p o e t/Shutterstock.com, 27, 28; ©Annette Shaff/Shutterstock.com, 27; ©Samuel Borges Photography/Shutterstock.com, 28; ©Eugenio Marongiu/Shutterstock.com, 29; ©AsyaPozniak/Shutterstock.com, 29; ©radFX/Shutterstock.com, 30; ©Hirurg/Shutterstock.com, 30; ©Dean Drobot/Shutterstock.com, 31; ©Vikram Raghuvanshi/iStockphoto, 31

Graphic Element Credits: ©Silhouette Lover/Shutterstock.com, back cover, multiple interior pages; ©Arevik/Shutterstock.com, back cover, multiple interior pages; ©tukkki/Shutterstock.com, multiple interior pages; ©paprika/Shutterstock.com, 24

**45th Parallel Press** is an imprint of Cherry Lake Publishing.

Library of Congress Cataloging-in-Publication Data

Names: Rowe, Brooke, author.
Title: What's your superpower? / Brooke Rowe.
Description: Ann Arbor : Cherry Lake Publishing, [2016] | Series: Best quiz ever | Includes index.
Identifiers: LCCN 2016001591| ISBN 9781634711081 (hardcover) | ISBN 9781634712071 (pdf) |
    ISBN 9781634713061 (pbk.) | ISBN 9781634714051 (ebook)
Subjects: LCSH: Ability—Miscellanea—Juvenile literature. | Superheroes—Miscellanea—Juvenile literature. |
    Personality tests—Juvenile literature.
Classification: LCC BF723.A25 R69 2016 | DDC 153.9--dc23
LC record available at http://lccn.loc.gov/2016001599

Printed in the United States of America
Corporate Graphics

# Table of Contents

Introduction ...................................... 4

To Take the Best Quiz Ever ..................... 5

Questions ........................................ 6

Solutions ....................................... 30

Glossary ........................................ 32

Index ........................................... 32

# Introduction

Hey! Welcome to the Best Quiz Ever series. This is a book. Duh. But it's also a pretty awesome quiz. Don't worry. It's not about math. Or history. Or anything you might get graded on. Snooze.

This is a quiz all about YOU.

# To Take the Best Quiz Ever:

Answer honestly!
Keep track of your answers. But don't write in the book!
(Hint: Make a copy of this handy chart.)
Don't see the answer you want? Pick the closest one.
Take it alone. Take it with friends!
Have fun! Obviously.

Question 1 _____       Question 7 _____

Question 2 _____       Question 8 _____

Question 3 _____       Question 9 _____

Question 4 _____       Question 10 _____

Question 5 _____       Question 11 _____

Question 6 _____       Question 12 _____

To get a copy of this activity, visit
www.cherrylakepublishing.com/activities.

# Pop quiz! What's your strategy?

**A.** Sneak away to the bathroom

**B.** Think! Think! Think!

**C.** Power through as fast as I can

**D.** Stare out the window

## Did you know?
Some people think the taste and smell of **peppermint** can help you do well on a test.

# What would be your ideal day in gym class?

**A.** Dodgeball

**B.** Capture the flag

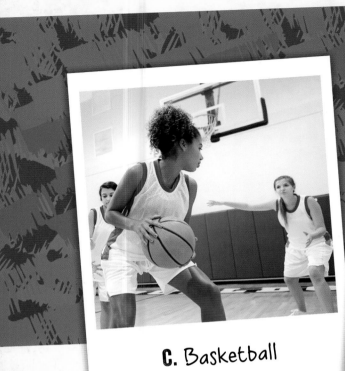

**C.** Basketball

**D.** Horseback riding

## Did you know?

A Michigan school won the National
Dodgeball Championship every
year from 2007 to 2015.

# Halloween's tomorrow?! You'll go as a:

**A. Ghost**

**B. Fortune-teller**

**C.** Zombie football star

**D.** Lion tamer

## Did you know?

Ghost hunters prefer to be called
paranormal investigators.

# School is tough. What's the best way to chill out?

**A.** Taking a nap

**B.** Chatting with a friend

**C.** Going for a long run

**D.** Catching frogs
at the pond

## Did you know?
Many frogs pee when they get scared.

# What do you argue about with your siblings?

**A.** Who broke Mom's iPhone

**B.** Who tattled

**C.** Who can run the fastest

**D.** Who the dog loves most

## Did you know?

Roger Bannister was the first person
to run a mile in under 4 minutes.
He did it in 1954.

# Your favorite movie is full of:

**A.** Mystery and suspense

**B.** Interesting characters

C. Thrilling adventures

D. Awesome animals

## Did you know?
The movie Star Wars: The Force Awakens
made $119.1 million in a single day
in December 2015.

# In this year's school yearbook, you would get the award for:

**A.** Best prankster

**B.** Friendliest

**C.** Most athletic

**D.** Finding the principal's dog

## Did you know?

*More than 7 million kids in the United States play soccer.*

# One thing you would NEVER do is:

**A.** Burp loudly in study hall

**B.** Post embarrassing pictures online

**C.** Skip the Super Bowl

**D.** Yell at a pet

## Did you know?

The most expensive Super Bowl commercial of all time was 2 minutes long and cost $12.4 million. It was for cars made by Chrysler.

# The coolest job ever would be:

**A.** Magician

**B.** Doctor

**C.** Pro wrestler

**D.** Marine biologist

# Did you know?

Many pro wrestlers wear masks to **conceal** their true identities.

# You're in trouble for late library books! You:

**A.** Avoid the library from now on

**B.** Convince the librarian to waive your fine

**C.** Turn them in and run away

**D.** Blame it on your dog

# Did you know?

Students have been saying "My dog ate my homework!" since the 1970s.

# Scavenger hunt! What's your strategy?

**A. Eavesdrop** on the other team

**B.** Think about the big picture

**C.** Run as fast as I can

**D.** Get my dog to sniff for clues

## Did you know?

In 2010, Forrest Fenn hid a treasure chest worth up to $3 million in the mountains of New Mexico. It still hasn't been found.

# Your favorite mode of transportation is:

**A.** Bus or train

**B.** Car

**C.** Walking

**D.** Horseback riding

## Did you know?
In the United States, about 30 million people ride horses every year.

You're done! Now you tally your score. Add up your As, Bs, Cs, and Ds. What letter do you have the most of? BTW, if you have a tie, you're a little bit of both.

### As: Invisibility

You're invisible! You can be very sly and sneaky. You love surprising your friends. And you always get away with every-thing. When you're not shocking your friends, you're blending in with the crowd. Just make sure you use your powers for good, not evil!

### Bs: Mind Reading

You're a mind reader! You can always guess what your friends are thinking. And you can ususally convince people to do whatever you want. Family and friends love telling you their problems. You give great advice. But remember, with great power comes great responsibility.

## Cs: Superhuman Strength

You're stronger than an ox! You're great at sports and very competitive. You usually win every race in gym class. You would play a school sport every season if you could. Devote yourself to a sport or two. You might just be the next Olympic star!

## Ds: Talking to Animals

You can talk to animals! Wild animals never seem afraid of you. And pets flock to you. Even when they're not your own. You always know just what they want. You love being outside, especially if that includes some wildlife sightings. Just be careful at the zoo. Some of those big animals might want to get too close for comfort!

# Glossary

**conceal (kuhn-SEEL)** to hide something

**convince (kuhn-VINS)** to make someone do or believe something

**eavesdrop (EEVZ-drahp)** to listen in on a conversation secretly

**peppermint (PEP-ur-mint)** a kind of mint plant used as flavoring

**waive (WAYV)** to give up or set aside

# Index

Bannister, Roger, 15

Chrysler, 21

Fenn, Forrest, 27
frogs, 13

ghost hunters, 11

horses, 29

National Dodgeball
    Championship, 9

peppermint, 7
pro wrestler, 23

soccer, 19
*Star Wars: The Force
    Awakens,* 17
Super Bowl, 21